What's behind that CLOUD?

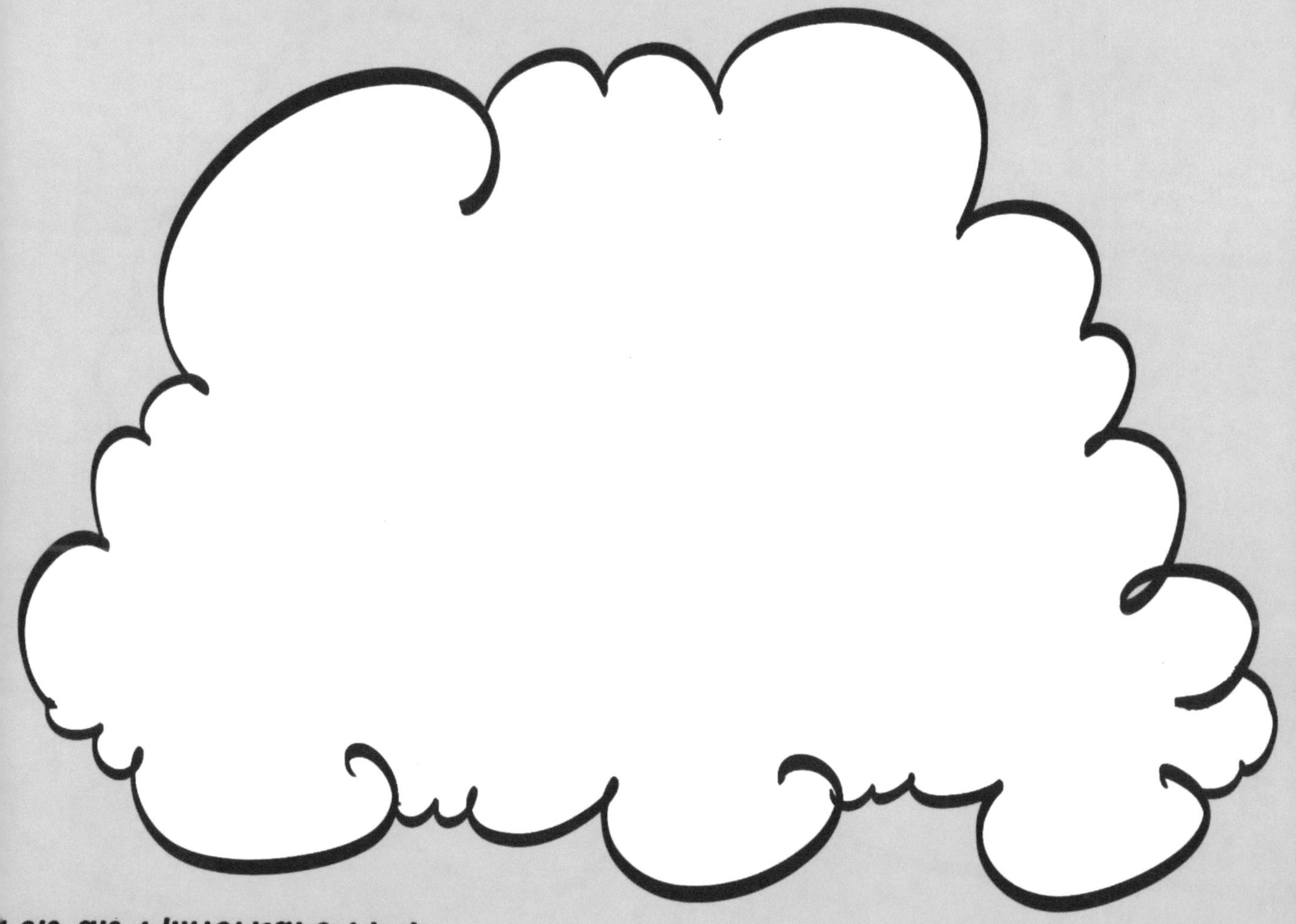

Written and Illustrated by:
Marie Lillge the Italic Illustrator

What's behind that CLOUD?

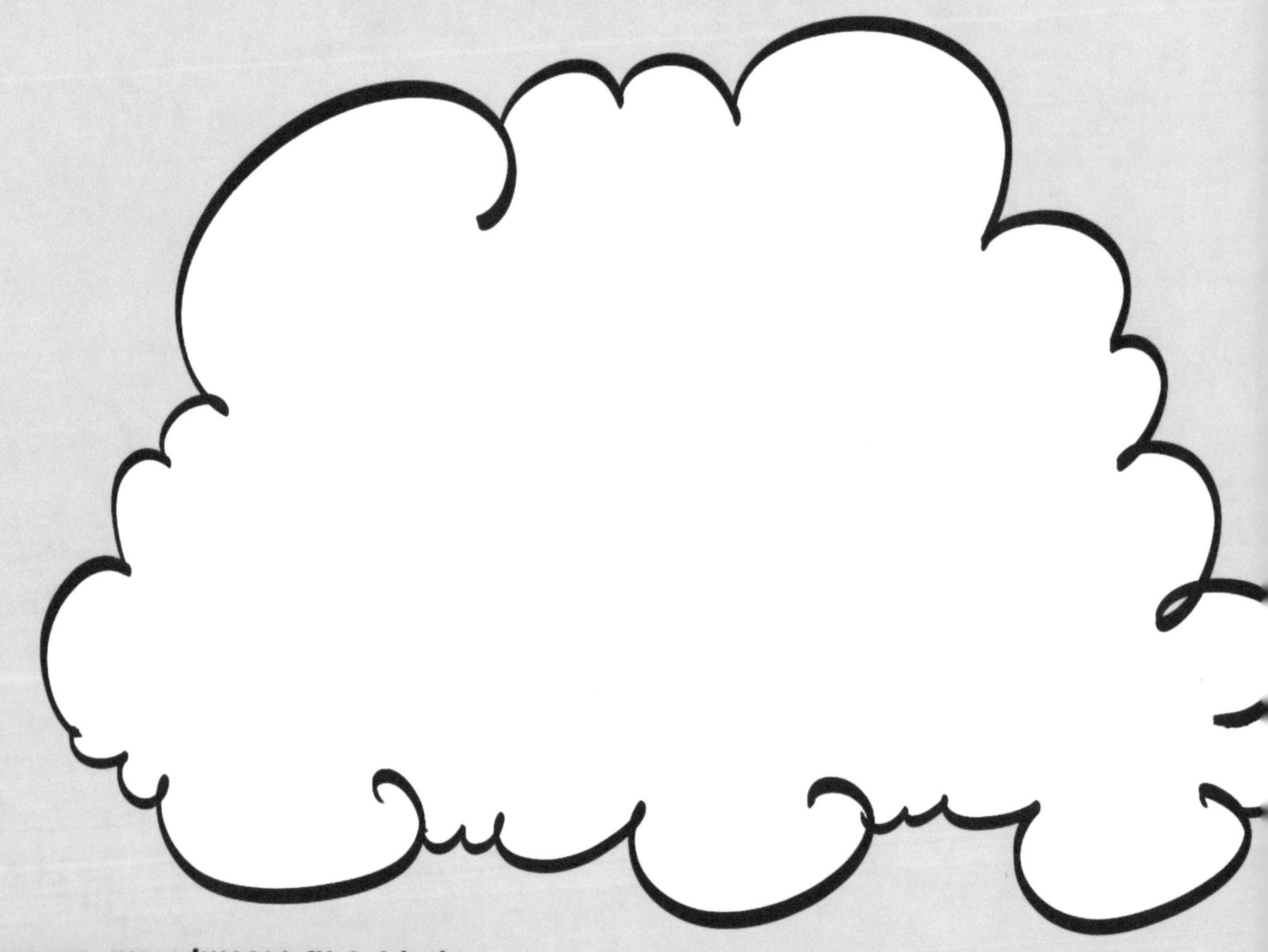

Written and Illustrated by:
Lynne Lillge the Italic Illustrator

3 Kiddos Publishing
What's Behind That Cloud

Distributed in partnership with
3 Kiddos Publishing

Http://www.3kiddospublishing.com

ISBN:9798988179405

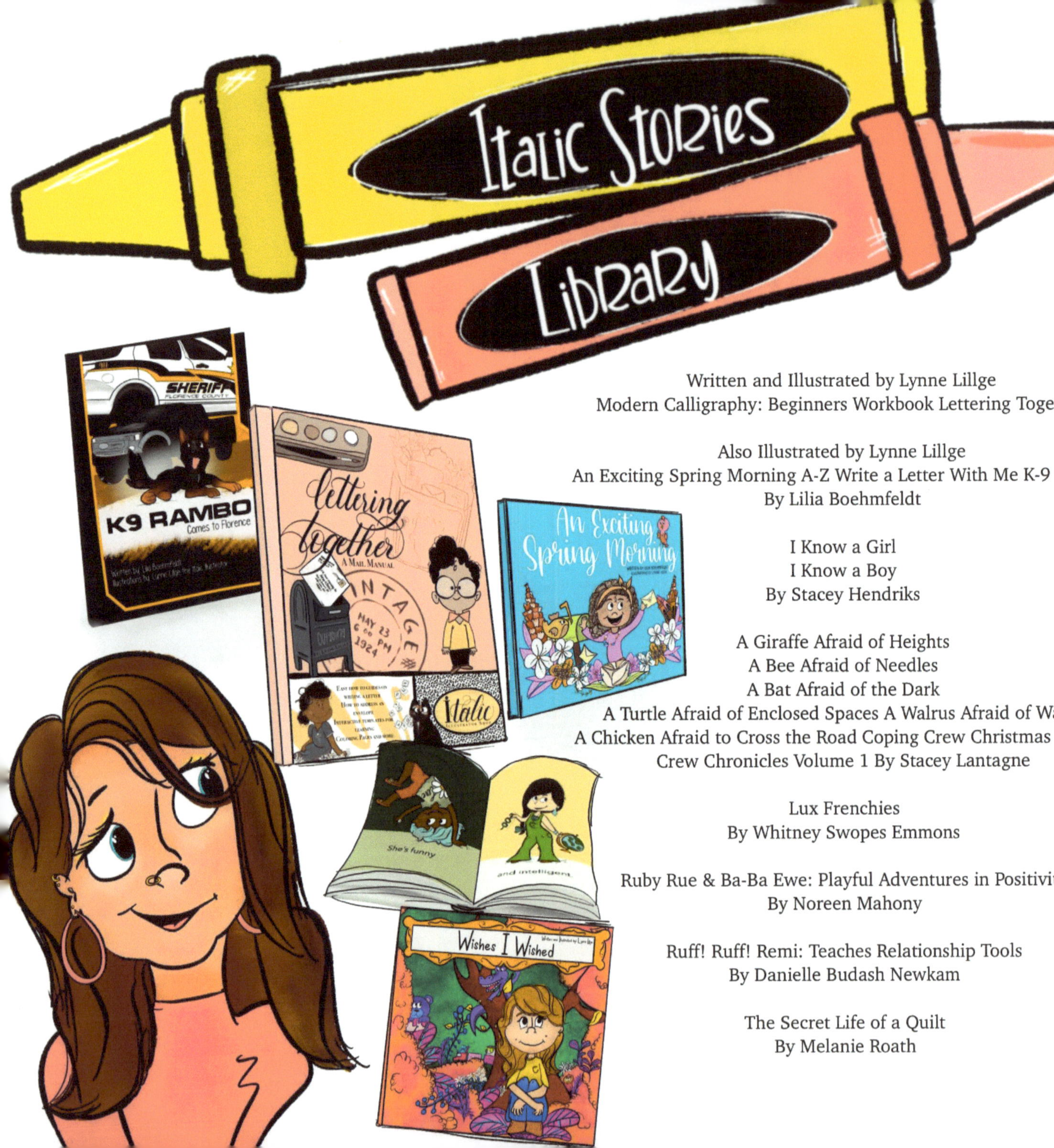
Italic Stories Library
Written and Illustrated by Lynne Lillge
Modern Calligraphy: Beginners Workbook Lettering Together
Also Illustrated by Lynne Lillge
An Exciting Spring Morning A-Z Write a Letter With Me K-9 Rambo
By Lilia Boehmfeldt
I Know a Girl
I Know a Boy
By Stacey Hendriks
A Giraffe Afraid of Heights
A Bee Afraid of Needles
A Bat Afraid of the Dark
A Turtle Afraid of Enclosed Spaces A Walrus Afraid of Water
A Chicken Afraid to Cross the Road Coping Crew Christmas
Crew Chronicles Volume 1 By Stacey Lantagne
Lux Frenchies
By Whitney Swopes Emmons
Ruby Rue & Ba-Ba Ewe: Playful Adventures in Positivity
By Noreen Mahony
Ruff! Ruff! Remi: Teaches Relationship Tools
By Danielle Budash Newkam
The Secret Life of a Quilt
By Melanie Roath

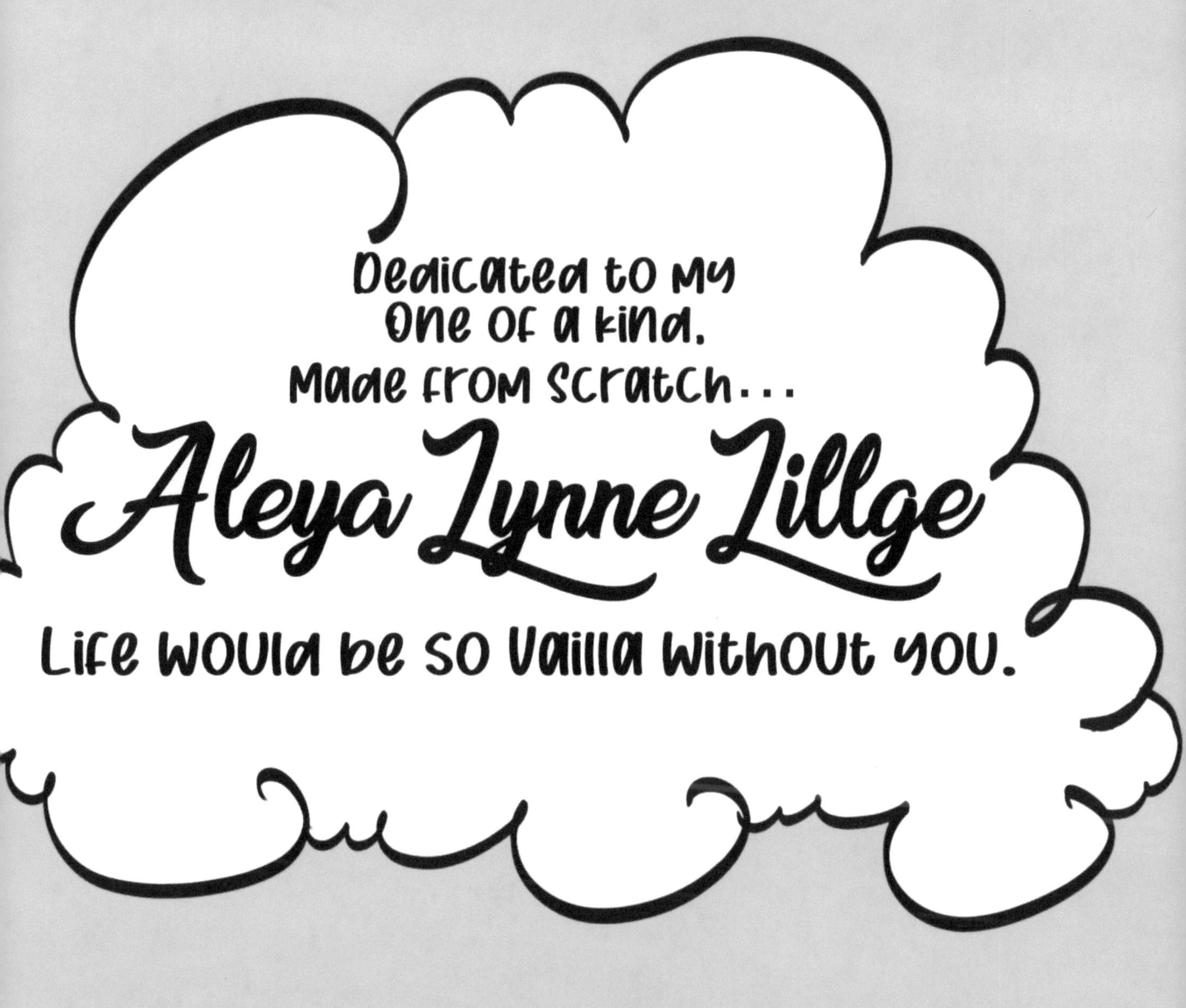

Dedicated to my
One of a kind,
Made from scratch...
Aleya Lynne Lillge
Life would be so vailla without you.

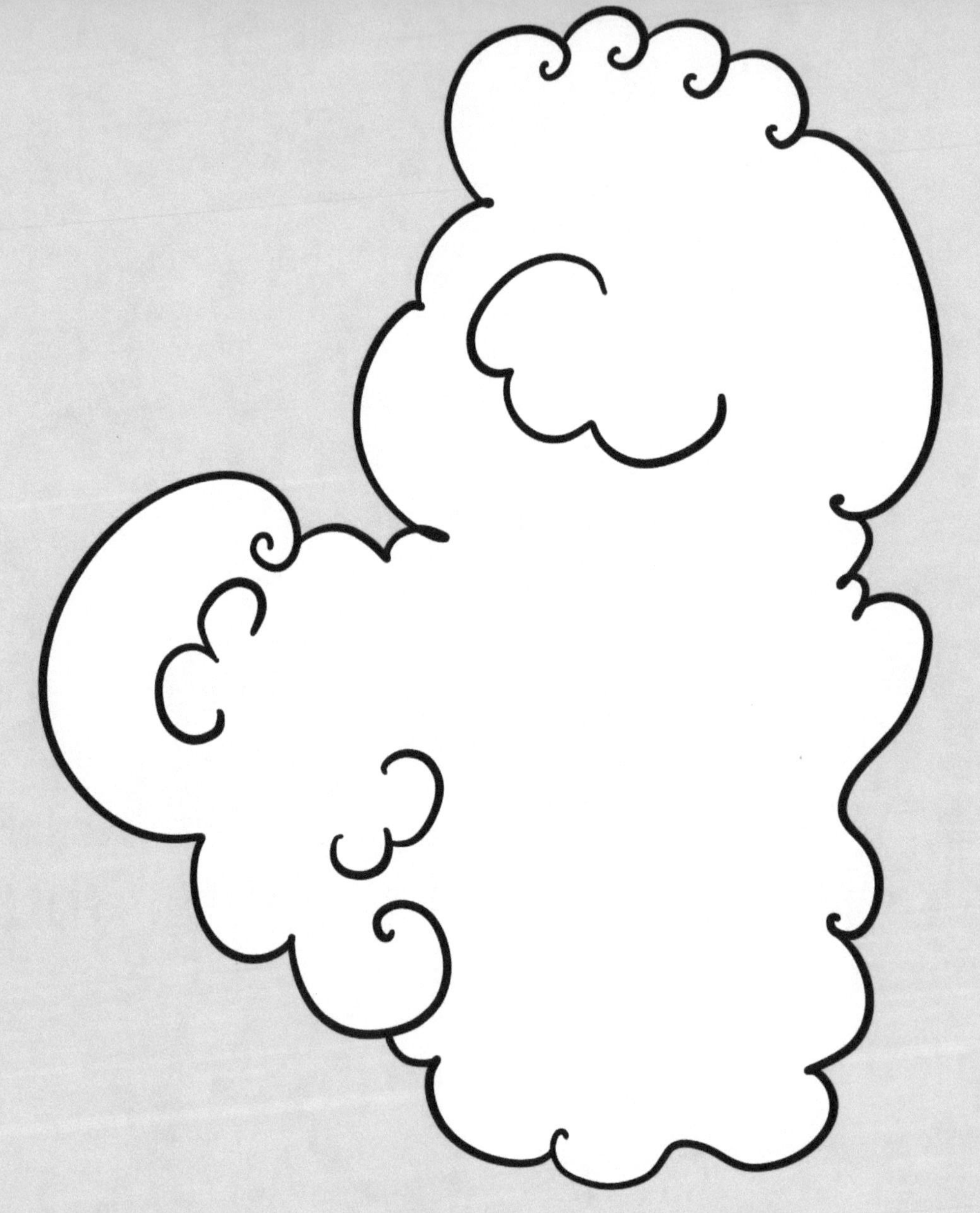

What's behind that **CLOUD?**

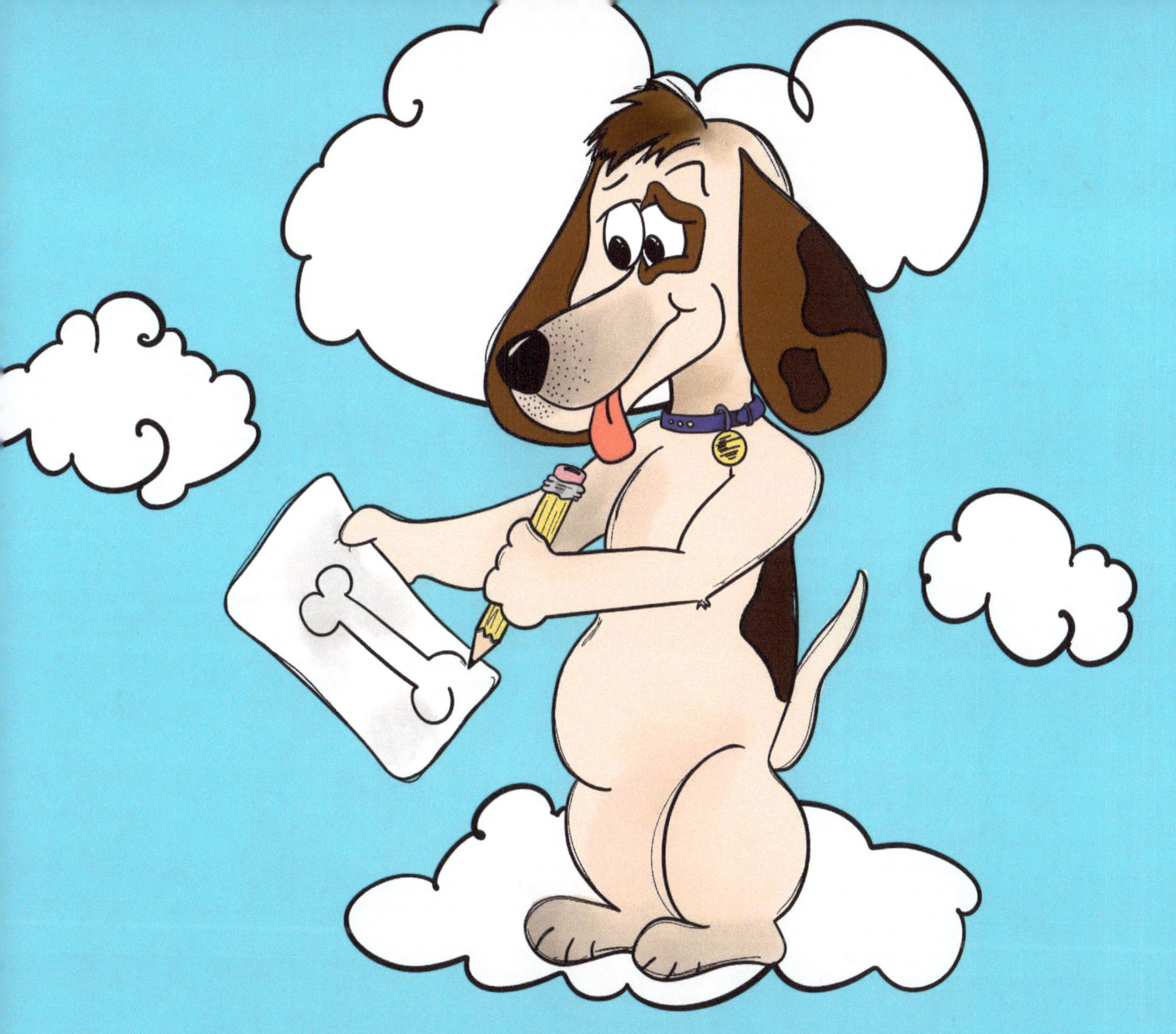

It's a dog named Noodle,
drawing a little doodle.

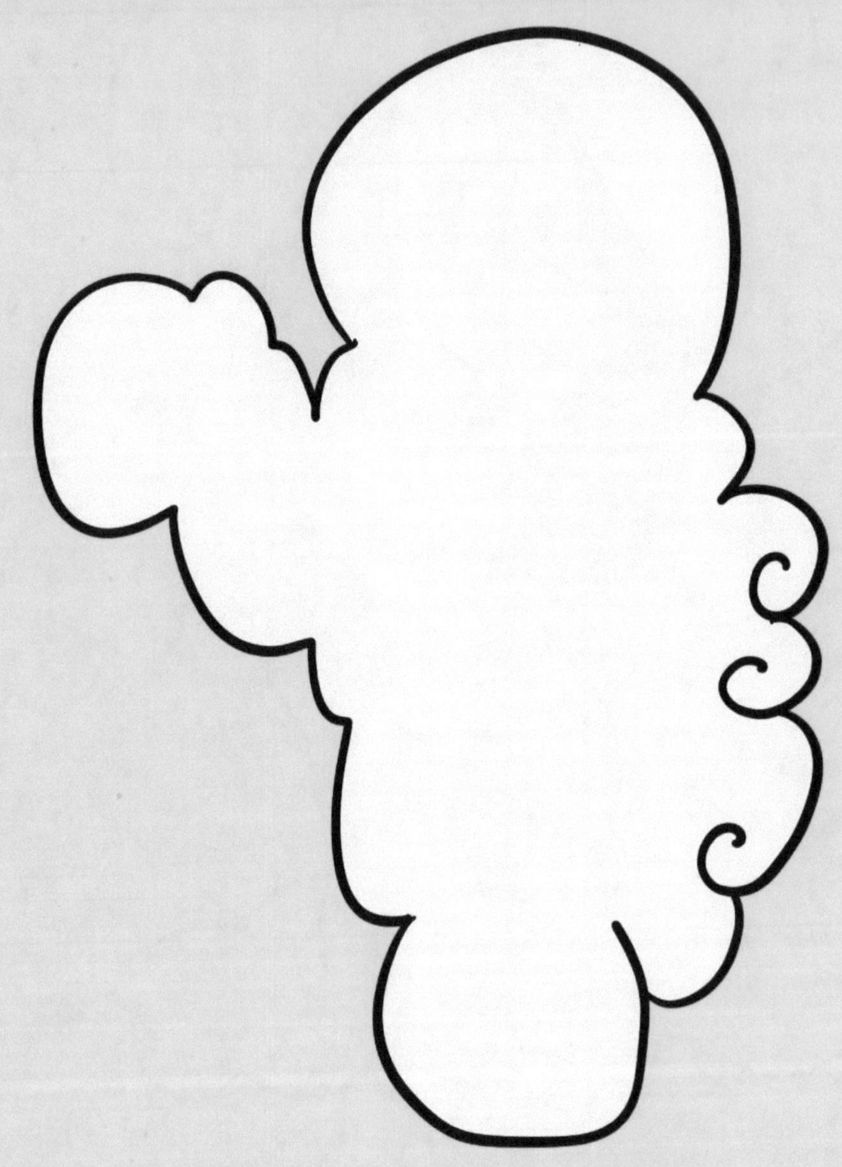

What's behind that CLOUD?

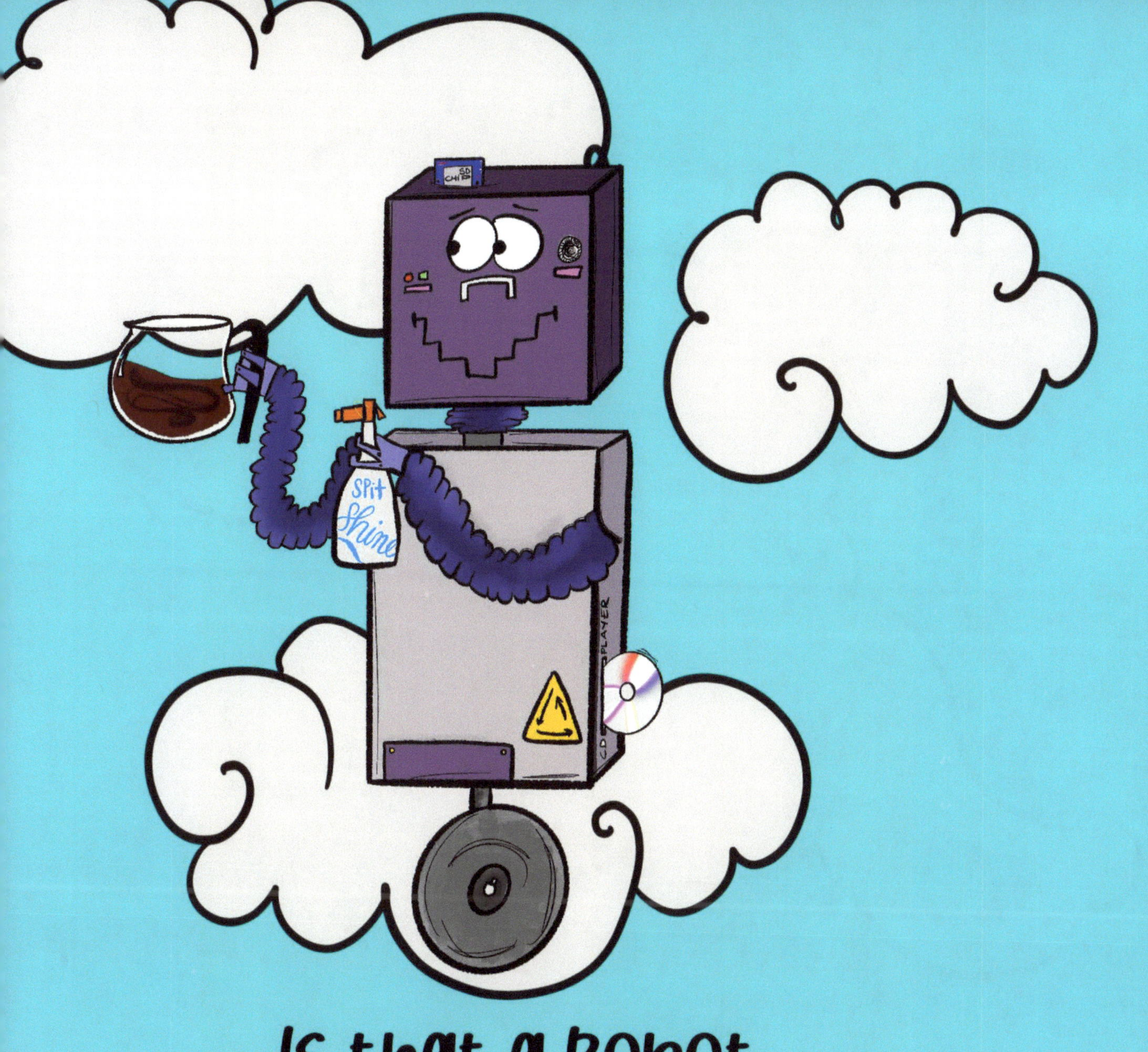

Is that a Robot
cleaning a Coffee Pot?

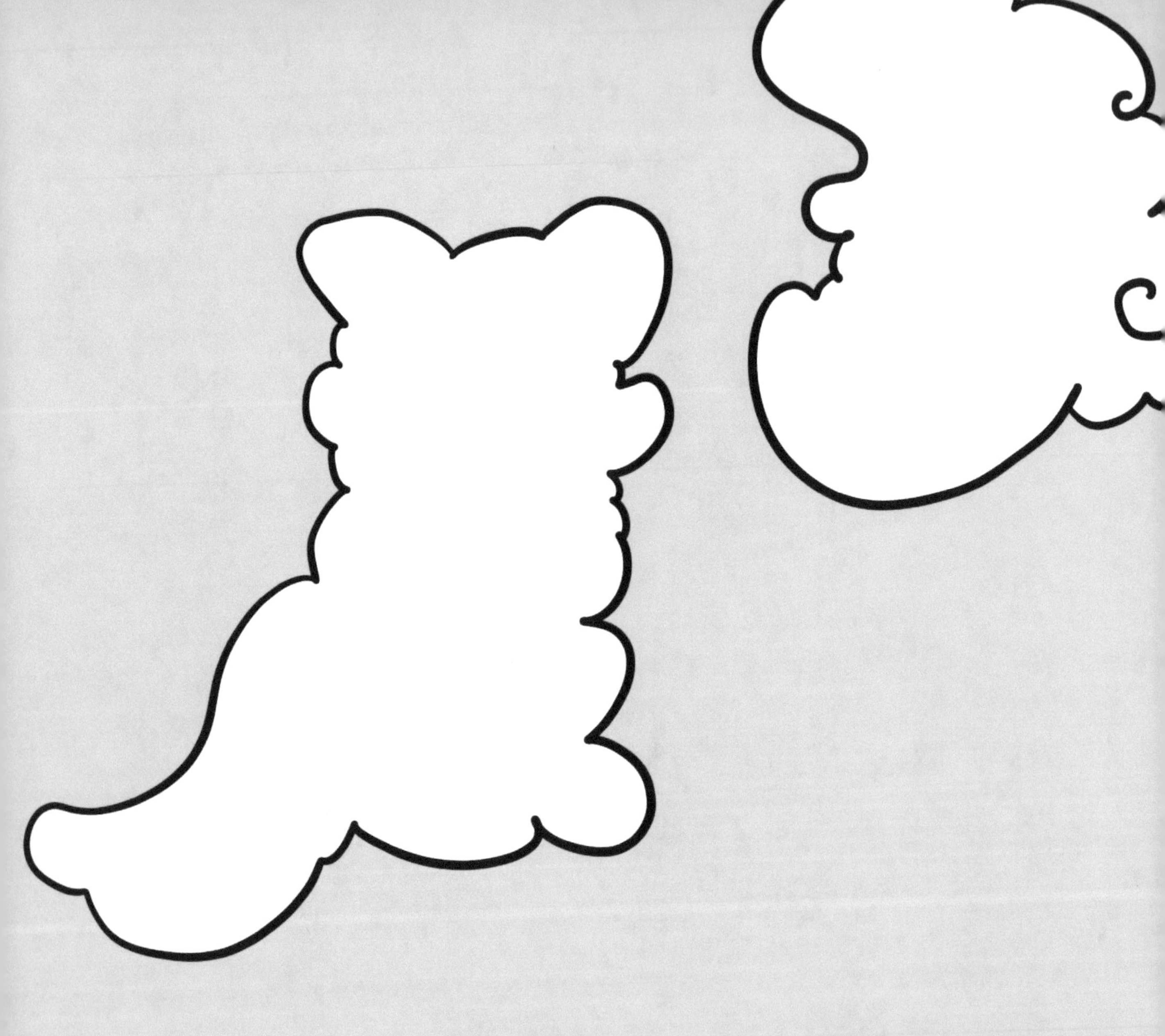

What's behind that **CLOUD?**

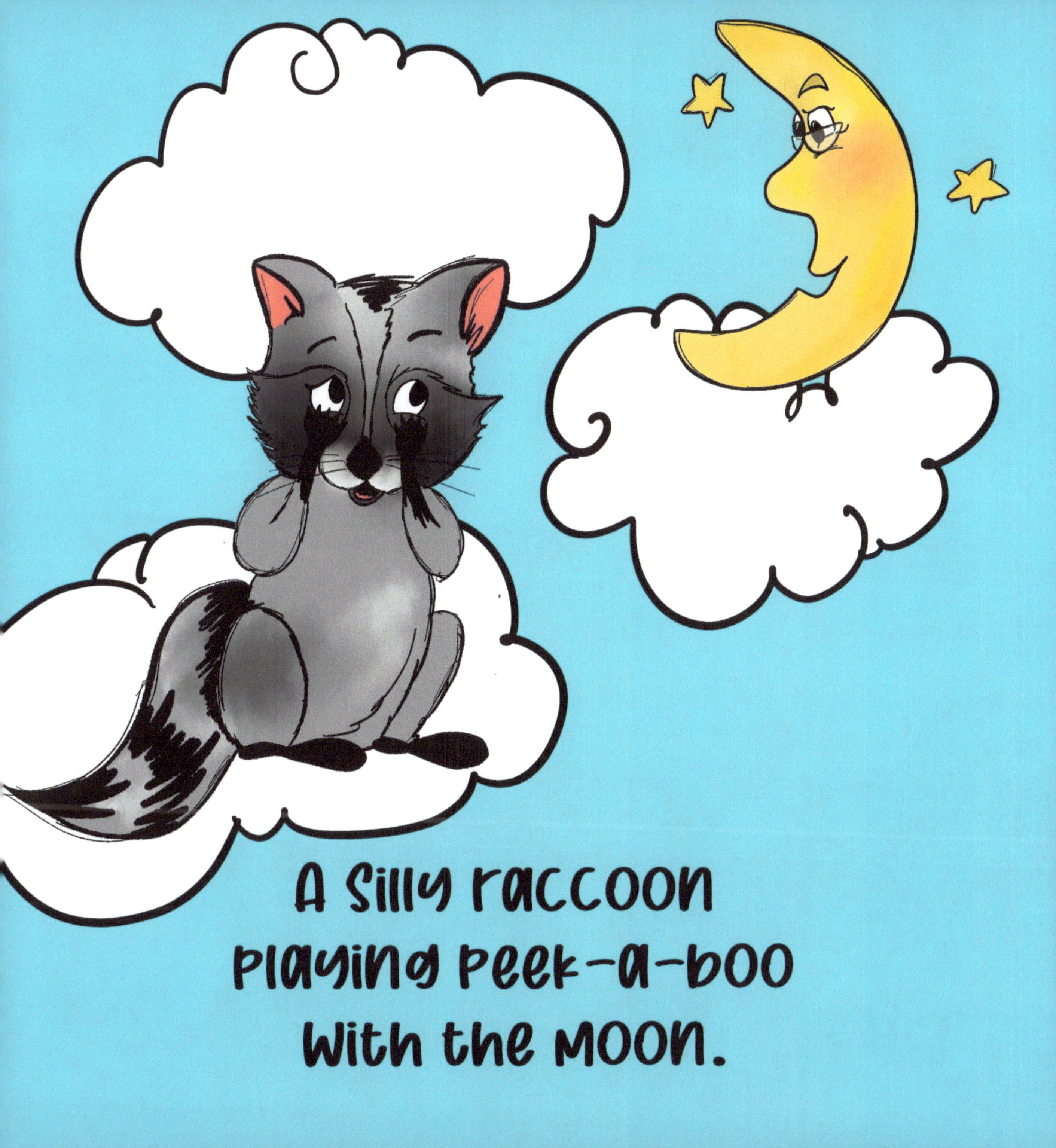
A silly raccoon
playing peek-a-boo
with the moon.

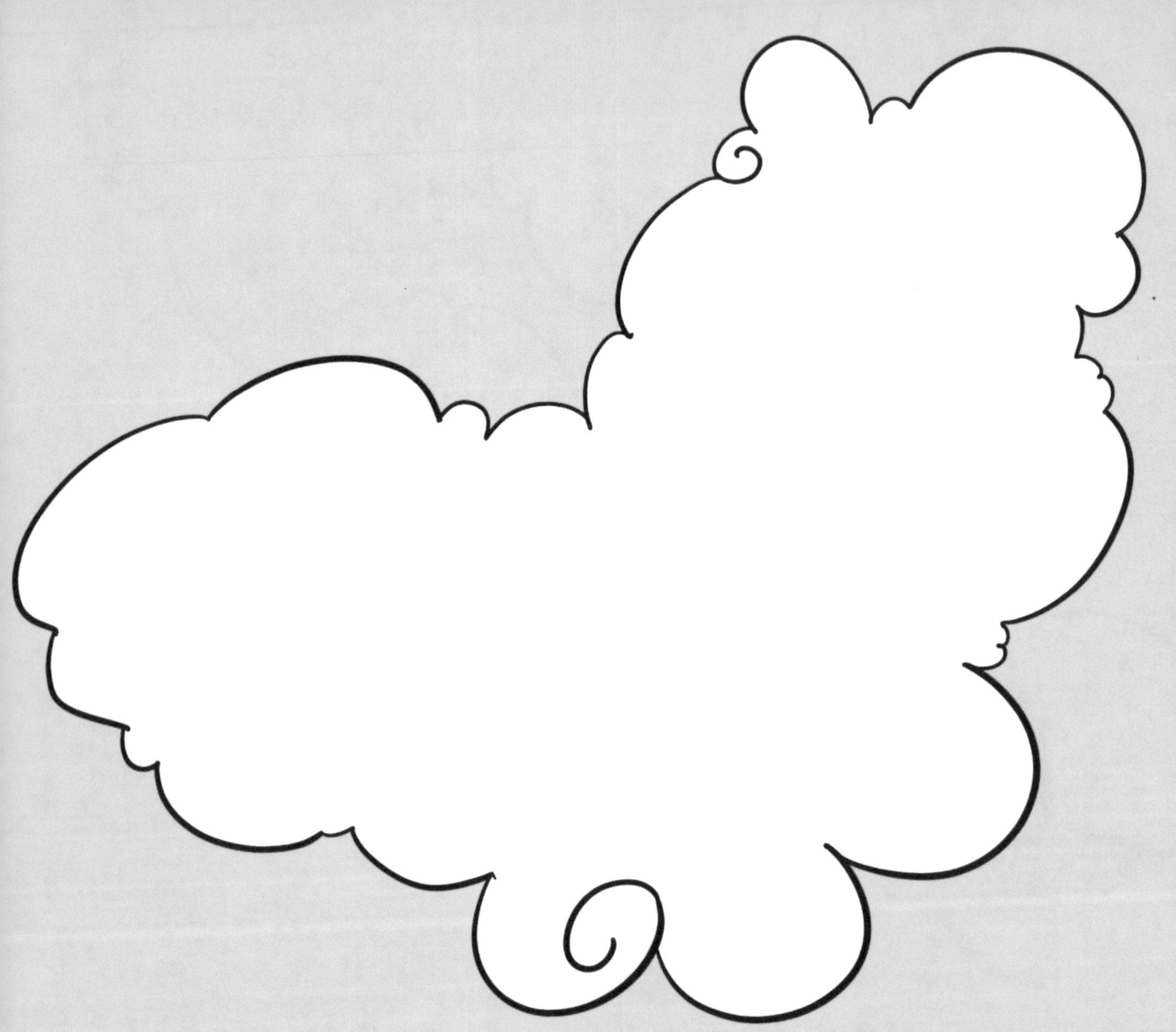

What's behind that **CLOUD?**

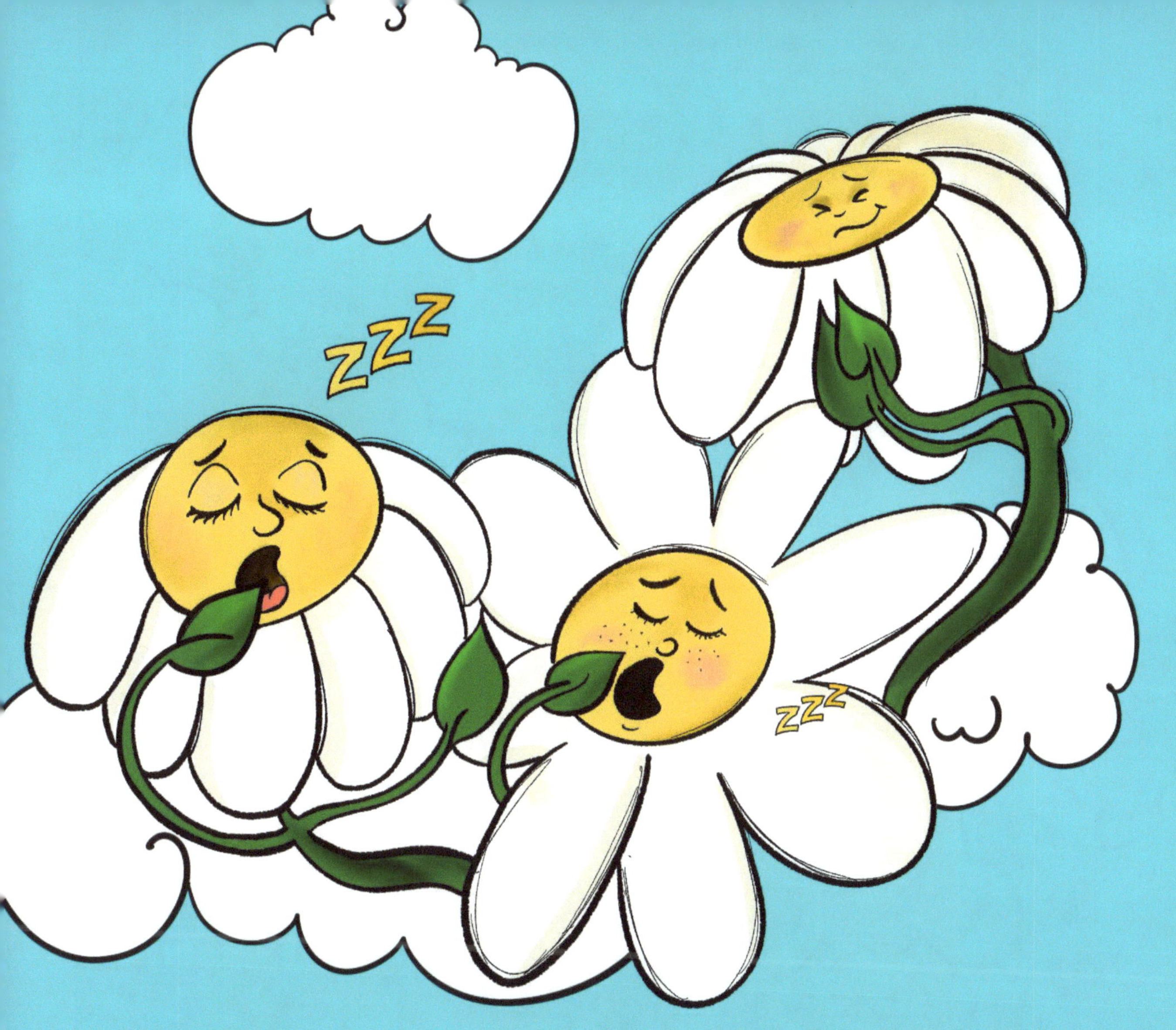

Looks like a field of Daisies ,
all being a little Lazy.

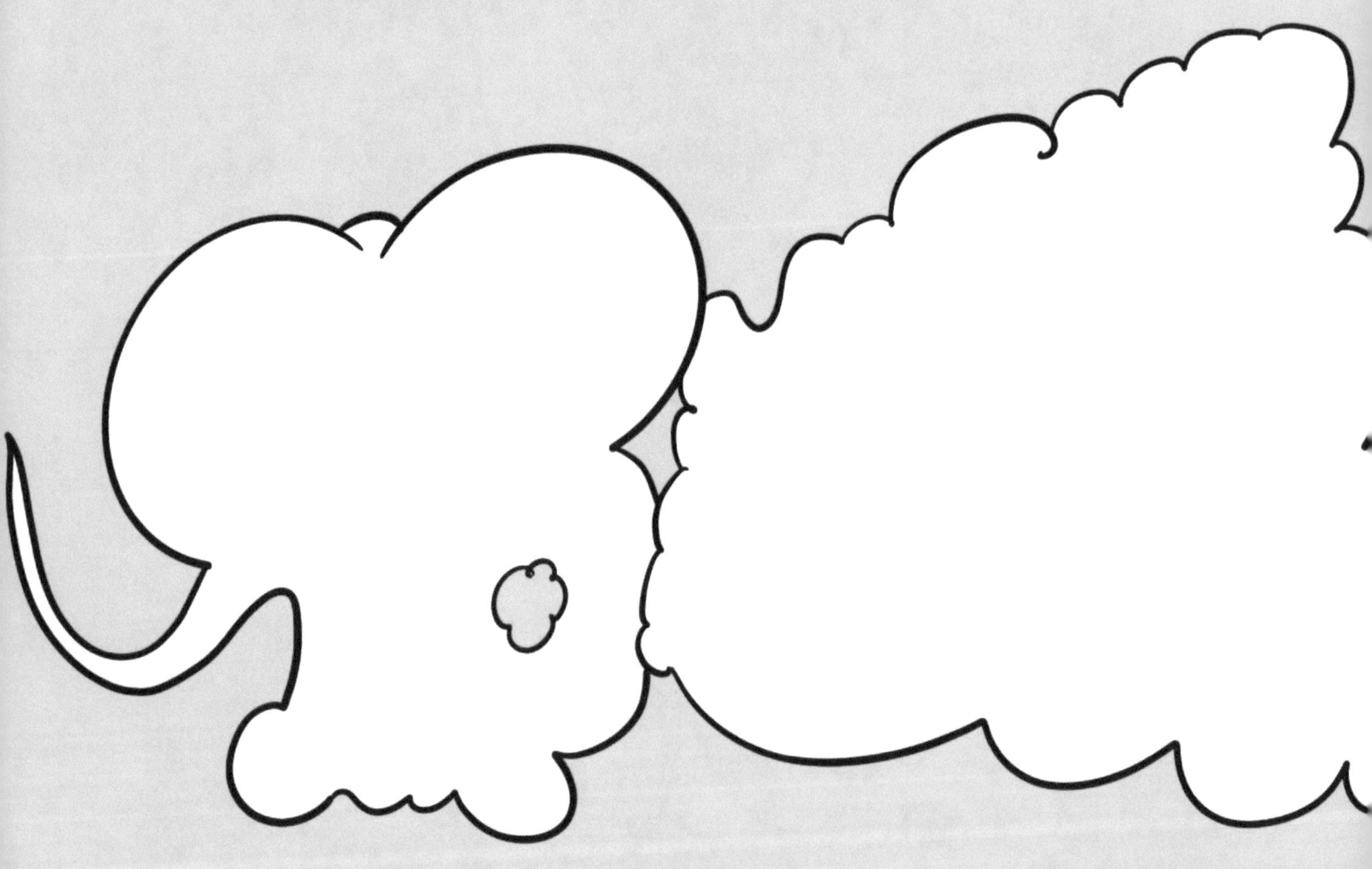

What's behind that **CLOUD?**

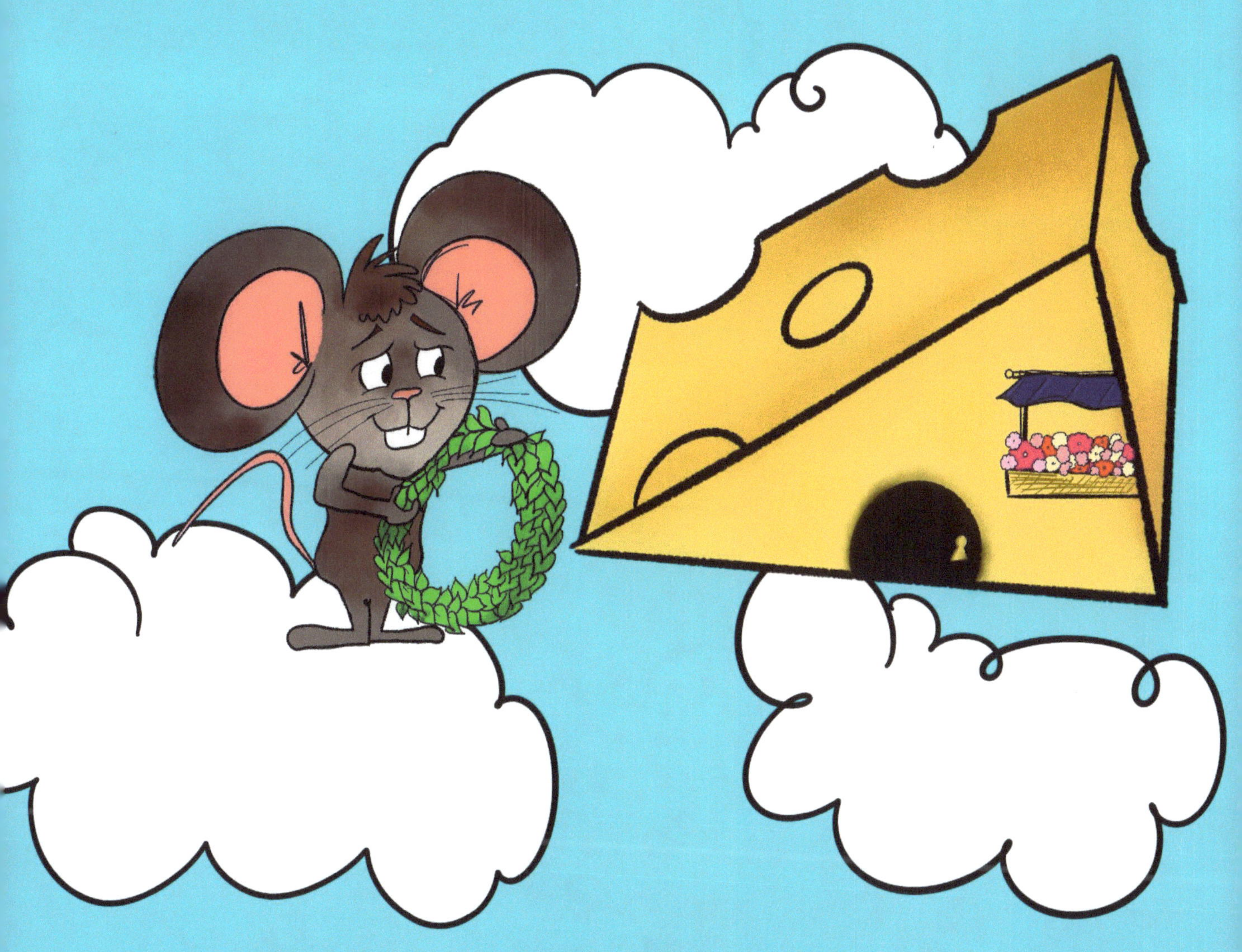
Oh! A litle mouse,
decorating his house!

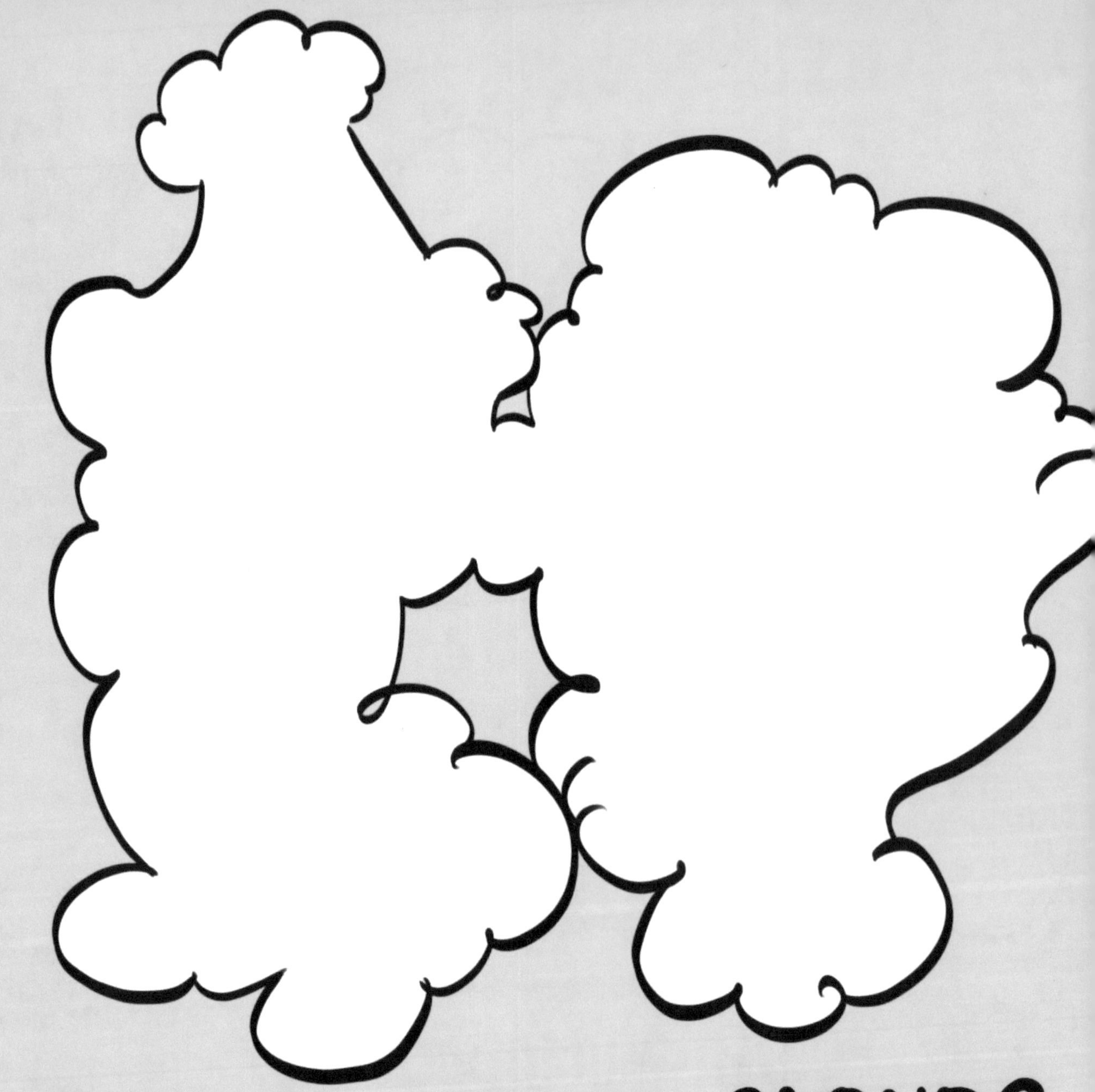

What's behind that **CLOUD?**

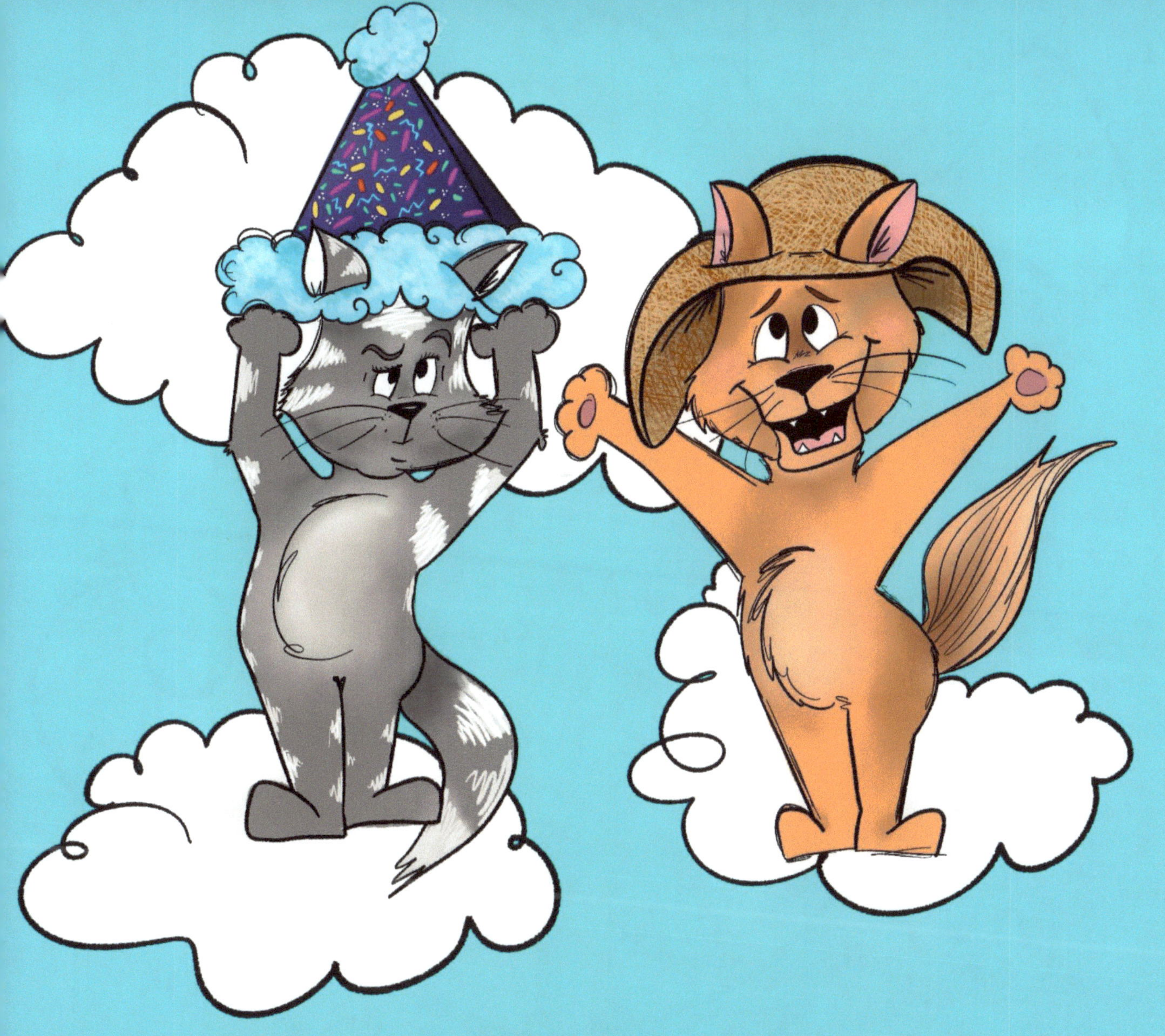

It's a couple of cats
trying on some fancy hats

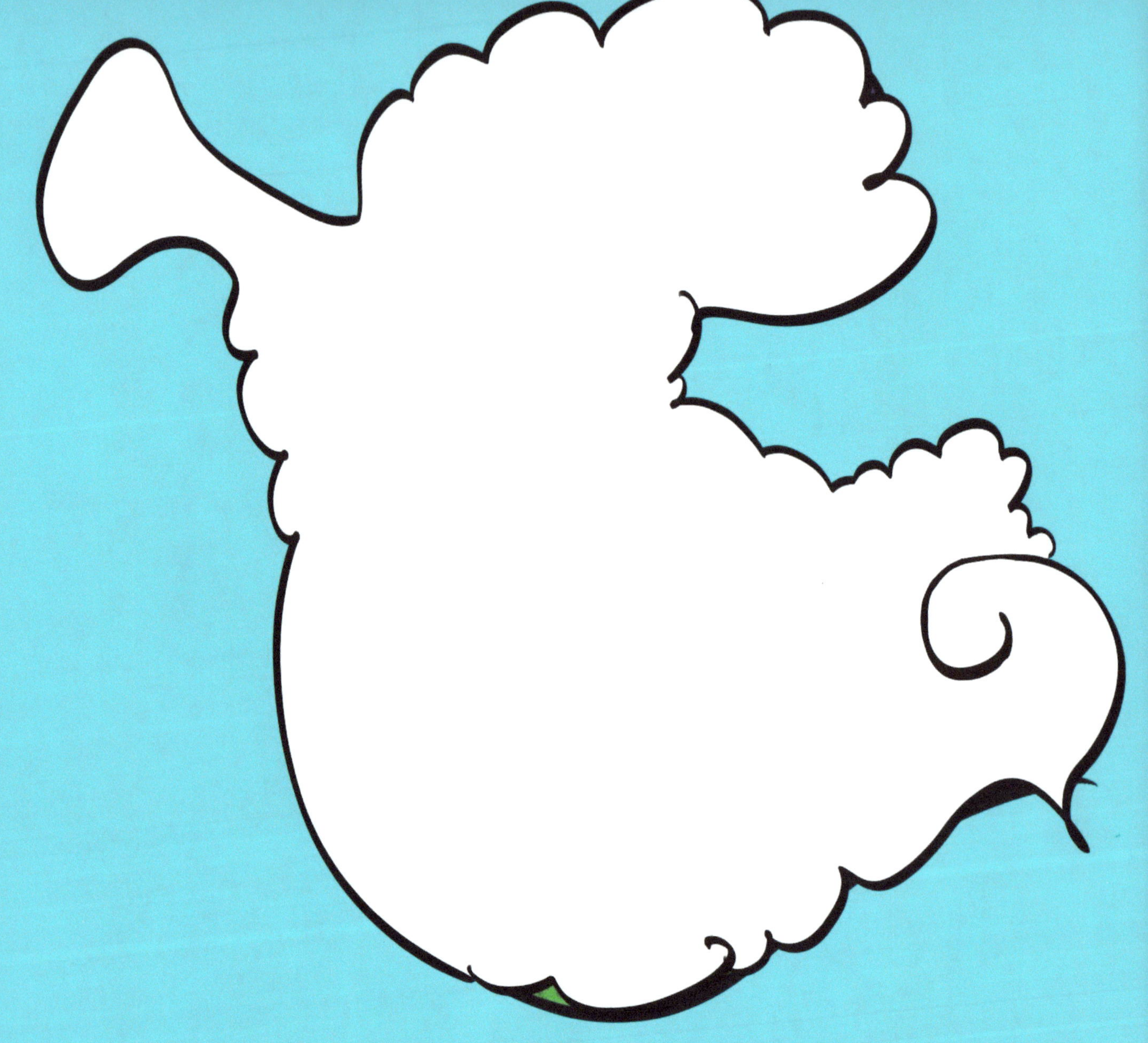

What's behind that CLOUD?

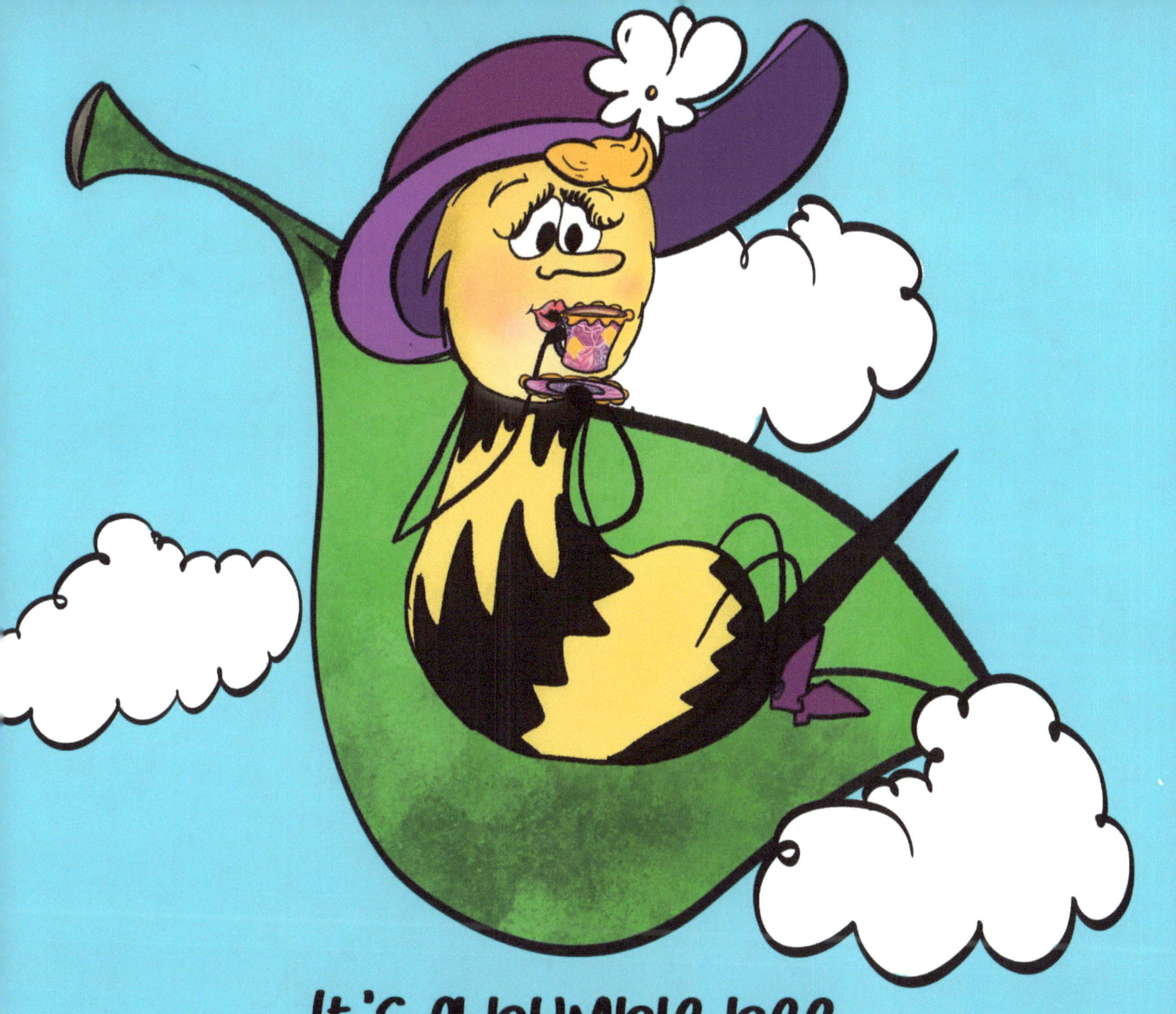

It's a bumble bee
sipping on a cup
of sweet tea.

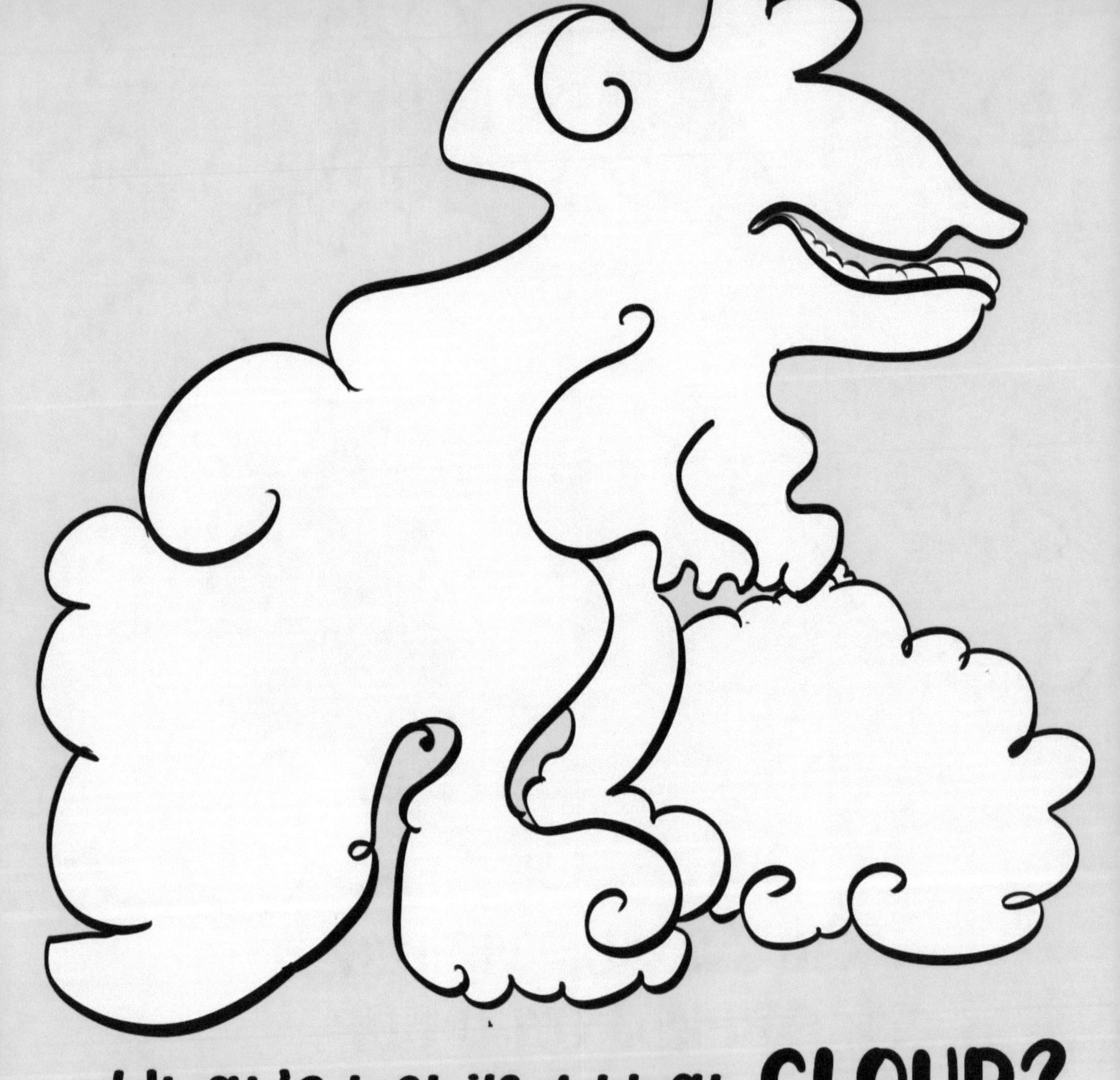

What's behind that **CLOUD?**

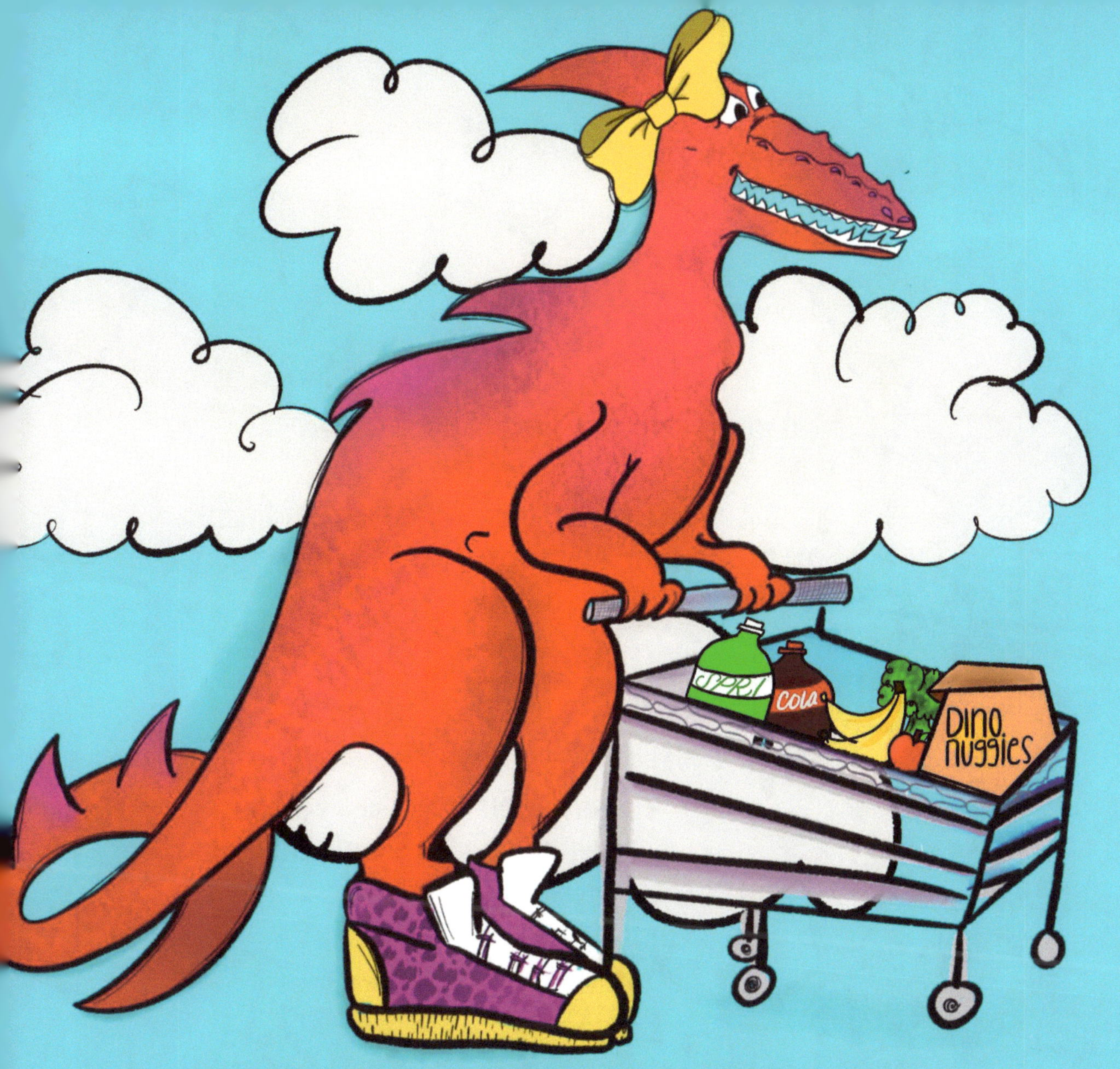

A dinosaur shopping
at a grocery store.

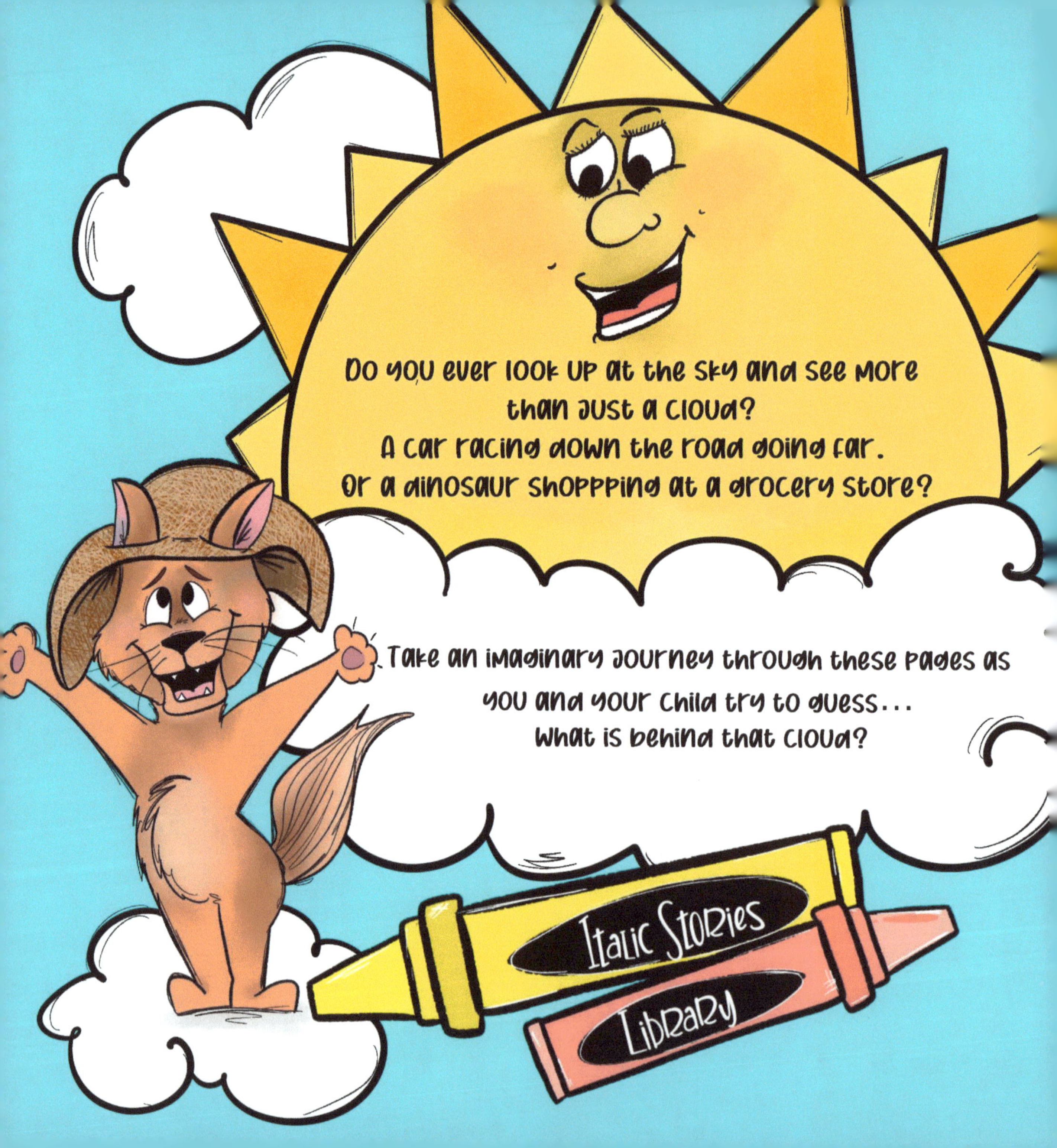

Do you ever look up at the sky and see more than just a cloud?
A car racing down the road going far.
Or a dinosaur shoppping at a grocery store?

Take an imaginary journey through these pages as you and your child try to guess...
What is behind that cloud?

Italic Stories
Library